ICAEW
Accounting

For exams in 2023

First edition 2007, Sixteenth edition 2022

ISBN 9781 0355 0186 1

British Library Cataloguing-in-Publication Data

A catalogue record for this publication is available from the British Library

Published by

BPP Learning Media Ltd
BPP House, Aldine Place
142-144 Uxbridge Road
London W12 8AA

www.bpp.com/learningmedia

Printed in the United Kingdom

Your learning materials, published by BPP Learning Media Ltd, are printed on paper obtained from traceable sustainable sources.

Welcome to BPP Learning Media's **Passcards** for ICAEW **Accounting**.

- They **save you time**. Important topics are summarised for you.

- They incorporate **diagrams** to kick start your memory.

- They follow the overall **structure** of the ICAEW Workbook, but BPP Learning Media's ICAEW **Passcards** are not just a condensed book. Each card has been separately designed for clear presentation. Topics are self-contained and can be grasped visually.

- ICAEW **Passcards** are **just the right size** for pockets, briefcases and bags.

- ICAEW **Passcards focus on the exams** you will be facing.

Run through the **Passcards** as often as you can during your final revision period. The day before the exam, try to go through the **Passcards** again! You will then be well on your way to passing your exams.

Good luck!

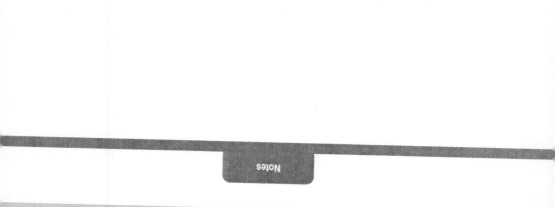

Notes

1: Introduction to accounting

This chapter looks at why financial statements are prepared.

Here we look at how the structure of accounting information has developed and how it may carry on developing.

Modern accounting is based on certain concepts and conventions.

We review the regulatory environment and the need for an ethical underpinning. We will also look at the development of sustainability standards, which is a major development in the profession.

We also look at the distinction between capital and revenue expenditure.

The purpose of accounting information	The regulation of accounting and ethical standards	Sustainability standards	The main financial statements	Qualitative characteristics of accounting information

Accounting is a way of recording, analysing and summarising the transactions of an entity.

There are three main types of profit-making business entity

Sole trader
The sole trader owns his or her own business. They may have employees.

Partnership
Two or more people may go into business together, sharing risks and rewards. Examples are accounting firms, solicitors, dentists.

Limited liability company
Limited liability companies are owned by their shareholders and managed by directors. The company itself is a separate legal entity.

Who needs financial information?

In the case of limited liability companies, especially listed companies, there is a wide group of users.

Users of accounts

Managers of the company

Shareholders of the company

Trade contacts

Providers of finance to the company

Taxation authorities (HMRC)

Employees of the company

Financial analysts and advisors

Government and their agencies

The public

The larger the entity, the greater the interest from various groups of people.

User information needs:

- Users need information in order to make decisions relating to providing resources to an entity

Users need to assess:

- The resources of an entity, claims against those resources and changes in the resources and claims
- How efficiently and effectively management have discharged their responsibilities
- The sustainability of an entity's operations and how an entity contributes to society

Ethical standards
IESBA Code of Ethics
ICAEW Code of Ethics

National law
Form and content of accounts may be regulated by national legislation.

Accounting standards
The IASB produces IFRS Standards. The IFRS Advisory Committee and IFRS Interpretations Committee help tackle issues/interpretation of standards.

Sustainability standards
The ISSB will develop disclosure standards focused on sustainability.

Influences upon financial accounting

Accounting concepts and individual judgement

GAAP
Drawn from:
- Local company law
- Accounting standards
- Statutory requirement in other countries
- Stock exchanges

Other international issues
see next page

International influences

- EU
- UN
- IESBA
- OECD

The international influence on accounting is very important. All listed companies in the UK have to prepare their consolidated accounts under International Financial Reporting Standards® (IFRS Standards).

Accounting standards

Developed at an international level by the IASB, they include:

- IFRS Standards
- IAS
- IFRIC Interpretations
- SIC interpretations

UK GAAP

Non-listed companies in the UK can choose IFRS Standards or UK Financial Reporting Standards (FRS). There are different IFRS Standards for different issues, but only one main accounting standard in the UK – FRS 102 – covering all issues.

ISSB was formed in 2021 to develop IFRS Sustainability Disclosure Standards.

The IFRS Sustainability Disclosure Standards will cover environmental, social and governance issues.

They will initially focus on climate-related issues.

IFRS Sustainability Disclosure Standards will sit alongside IFRS Standards.

Main financial statements

Statement of financial position

A list of assets controlled by the entity and liabilities owed by the entity on a particular date.

- Total assets = Total liabilities + equity
- Amount invested by owner is **equity** (capital).

Statement of profit or loss

A record of income generated and expenditure incurred over a given period.

The statement shows the entity's **financial position** at a given point in time.

The statement of profit or loss shows the entity's **financial performance** over a period of time.

Financial statements must give a 'true and fair view' or 'present fairly' the entity's financial position.

1: Introduction to accounting

The two fundamental qualitative characteristics defined by the *Conceptual Framework* are:

- Relevance - predictive or confirmatory value

- Faithful representation - complete, neutral (prudence), free from error

Relevant and faithfully represented information is enhanced by

- Timeliness
- Understandability
- Verifiability
- Comparability

IAS 1, *Presentation of Financial Statements* considers accounting policies, fundamental assumptions and the format and content of financial statements.

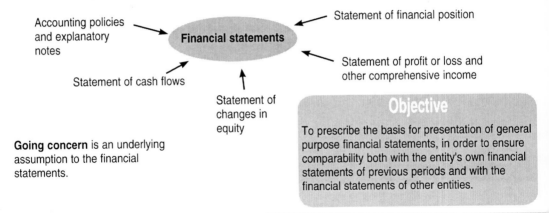

Accounting policies and explanatory notes

Financial statements

Statement of cash flows

Statement of changes in equity

Statement of financial position

Statement of profit or loss and other comprehensive income

Going concern is an underlying assumption to the financial statements.

Objective

To prescribe the basis for presentation of general purpose financial statements, in order to ensure comparability both with the entity's own financial statements of previous periods and with the financial statements of other entities.

Financial statements should **present fairly** financial performance, financial position and cash flows. Compliance with IFRS Standards will help to ensure this.

Going concern
The entity will continue in operation for the foreseeable future. There is no intention to put the entity into liquidation or to make drastic cutbacks to the scale of the operations.

Accruals
Revenue and costs must be recognised as they are earned or incurred, not as money is received or paid. They must be matched with one another and dealt with in the period in which they are incurred.

Business entity
The entity is separate from its assets.

Consistency
The presentation and classification of items should stay the same from one period to the next.

Materiality
Information is material if omitting, misstating or obscuring it could influence the economic decisions of users.

Historical cost
Transactions are recorded at the cost when they occurred.

Judgement is required in applying accounting concepts

The exercise of judgement in accounting matters should always be underpinned by **ethical principles**.

IESBA Code of Ethics for Professional Accountants

- **Integrity** - straightforward and honest in all relationships.

- **Objectivity** - do not allow bias, conflict of interest or undue influence of others to override judgements.

- **Professional competence and due care** - duty to maintain professional knowledge and skill, act diligently and in accordance with applicable standards.

- **Confidentiality** - respect the confidentiality of information acquired.

- **Professional behaviour** - comply with relevant laws and regulations and avoid any action that discredits the profession.

ICAEW Code of Ethics is a principles-based system

Capital expenditure

This results in the acquisition of non-current assets, or an increase in their earning capacity.

Revenue expenditure

This is incurred for the purpose of trade or to maintain the existing earning capacity of the non-current assets.

Examples

- Property purchase
- Vehicle purchases
- Plant and machinery purchases
- Cost of installing plant and machinery

Examples

- Property repairs
- Depreciation of assets
- Computer maintenance
- Travel costs
- Office expenses

2: The accounting equation

This chapter looks at the fundamental mechanics of financial statements and introduces the statement of financial position and statement of profit or loss.

The accounting equation will help you to see why the statement of financial position must balance.

The accounting equation:

$$\text{ASSETS} = \text{CAPITAL} + \text{LIABILITIES}$$

Profits

Excess of income over expenses

Profits are **added to** capital

Capital

Investment of funds with the intention of earning a return

Drawings

Amounts withdrawn from the business by the owner

Drawings **reduce** capital

The accounting equation is based on the principle that an entity is separate from the owner

Credit transactions give rise to:

Trade receivable

An asset: a balance owed to the business by a credit customer

A credit customer is also known as a **debtor**.

Trade payable

A liability: a balance owed by the business to a credit supplier

A credit supplier is also known as a **creditor**.

The statement of financial position

A list of assets, liabilities and capital of a business at a given moment.

Happiness
Statement of financial position
as at 31 August 20X1

ASSETS	£	£
Non-current assets		
Land and buildings		100,000
Fixtures and fittings		16,000
Motor vehicles		18,000
		134,000
Current assets		
Inventories	10,000	
Trade receivables	23,000	
Prepayments	100	
Cash	700	
		33,800
Total assets		167,800

Non-current assets are acquired for continuing use within the business for a period of more than one year.

Current assets are cash or assets that are expected to be converted into cash within one year.

EQUITY AND LIABILITIES
Equity

Capital as at 1 September 20X0		95,200
Profit for the year		16,000
		111,200
Less drawings		(8,000)
Capital as at 31 August 20X1		103,200
Non-current liabilities		
Loan		50,000
Current liabilities		
Bank overdraft	4,000	
Trade payables	3,600	
Taxation payable	7,000	
		14,600
		167,800

Non-current liabilities are payable after more than one year.

Current liabilities are payable within one year.

Capital + liabilities = assets

2: The accounting equation

The statement of profit or loss

This matches revenue earned in a period with the costs incurred in earning it.

This is known as the **accruals concept**.

Gross profit = revenue – cost of sales

Profit for the year = gross profit – expenses

Happiness – Statement of profit or loss for the year ended 31 August 20X1

	£	£
Revenue		80,000
Opening inventory	5,000	
Purchases	40,000	
Closing inventory	(10,000)	
Cost of goods sold		35,000
Gross profit		45,000
Less expenses		
Rent	12,000	
Depreciation	1,000	
Wages	12,000	
Other expenses	4,000	
		29,000
Profit for the year		16,000

3: Recording financial transactions

Topic List

Computerised accounting systems

Source documents

Cash at bank account

Petty cash

Payroll

This chapter covers the main sources of data and the function each source or record has.

We will see how the documents are recorded in the accounting records to reflect business transactions.

- Computerised accounting systems are commonplace in most businesses

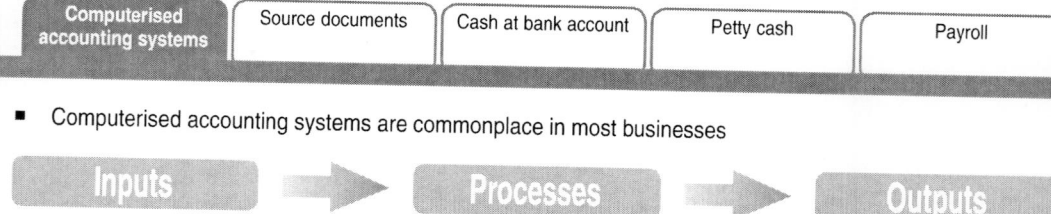

Inputs → **Processes** → **Outputs**

Inputs:
- Source documents
- Standing data

Processes:
- Ledgers
- Journals
- Calculations
- Record keeping

Outputs:
- Reports
- Trial balance
- Financial statements

- Software packages consist of 'ledgers' which capture the accounting information from the transactions businesses undertake
- Cloud accounting allows a business to access accounting records via the internet
- Assume a computerised accounting system is used, but need to consider the underlying principles and approach of a manual system to understand how a computerised system operates

Source documents

Business transactions are nearly always evidenced by a document. These documents are the source of the information in the accounts. Source documents you will see in *Accounting* are:

- Invoices (sales and purchases)
- Credit notes
- The bank transaction report

Businesses have constant access to online banking and will use bank information to update accounting records. Computerised accounting systems match transactions in the electronic bank statements to transactions in the accounting system.

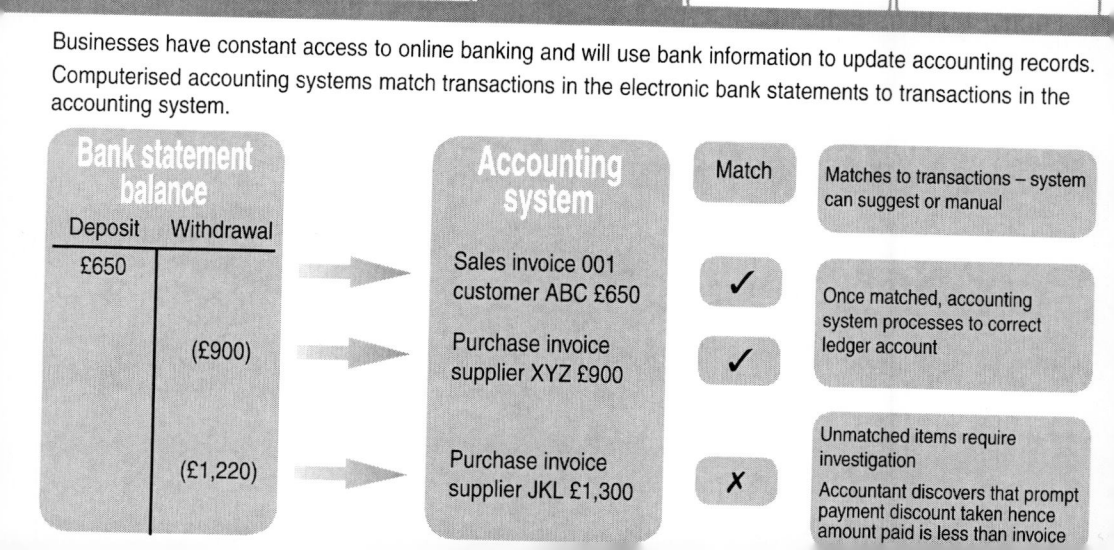

Petty cash

Most businesses keep a small amount of cash on the premises for small payments, eg, stamps, coffee. Petty cash payments and receipts are recorded in a petty cash book.

PETTY CASH

	RECEIPTS				PAYMENTS			
Date	Narrative	Total £	Date	Narrative	Total £	Stationery £	Coffee £	etc £
3.3.X9	Bank	50	3.3.X9	Paper	10	10		
				Coffee	5		5	
		50			15	10	5	

Under the 'imprest system':

	£
Cash still held in petty cash	X
Plus voucher payments	X
Must equal the imprest amount	X

Reimbursement is made equal to the voucher payments to bring the float back up to the imprest amount.

3: Recording financial transactions

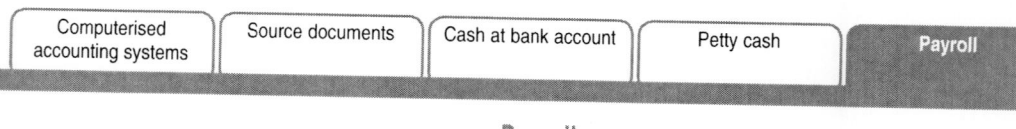

Payroll

Wages and salaries costs are entered into the accounting system from the payroll.

Payroll amounts break down as follows:

	£
Employee's gross pay	X
Employee's NI contribution	(X)
PAYE income tax	(X)
Employee's pension contribution	(X)
Balance paid to employee (net pay)	X

The employer will pay to HMRC:

	£
Employee's NI contribution	X
PAYE income tax	X
Plus employer's NI contribution	X
	X

4: Ledger accounting and double entry

Topic List

The nominal ledger

Double entry bookkeeping

Journal entries

Double entry for petty cash

The receivables and payables ledgers

Accounting for discounts

Accounting for VAT

This chapter looks at ledger accounting.

Information from source documents is recorded in ledger accounts. We will refer to the nominal ledger, the receivables ledger and the payables ledger. Transactions are recorded in the nominal ledger using double-entry bookkeeping.

VAT is a consumer expenditure tax. This is not a major part of the syllabus but it may come up as part of a larger question.

Ledger accounting

The process by which a business keeps a record of its transactions:

- In chronological order
- Built up in cumulative totals

A ledger account or 'T' account looks like this.

NAME OF ACCOUNT

	£		£
DEBIT SIDE		CREDIT SIDE	

The nominal ledger

The main accounting record in which accounting transactions are recorded. Accounts within the nominal ledger include the following.

- Plant and machinery (non-current asset)
- Inventories (current asset)
- Sales (income)
- Rent (expense)
- Trade payables (current liability)

Basic principles: dual effect

Double entry bookkeeping is based on the same idea as the accounting equation.

- Every accounting transaction has two equal but opposite effects.
- Equality of assets and liabilities is preserved.

In a system of double entry bookkeeping every accounting event must be entered in ledger accounts both as a debit and as an equal but opposite credit.

Debit	Credit
- An increase in an expense	- An increase in income
- An increase in an asset	- An increase in a liability
- A decrease in a liability	- A decrease in an asset

Double entry bookkeeping

The rules of double entry bookkeeping are best learnt by considering the cash at bank account.

- A **credit** entry indicates a payment made by the business; the matching debit entry is then made in an account denoting an expense paid, an asset purchased or a liability settled.
- A **debit** entry in the cash at bank account indicates cash received by the business; the matching credit entry is then made in an account denoting revenue received, a liability created or an asset realised.

Journal entry

Format of journal entries is as follows.

Date	Debit £	Credit £
DEBIT A/c to be debited	X	
CREDIT A/c to be credited		X

Narrative to explain transaction

Double entry for petty cash

The double entry for topping up the petty cash is as follows:

	£	£
DEBIT Petty cash	X	
CREDIT Cash at bank account		X

Petty cash is topped up to an agreed balance – the 'imprest amount'.

The receivables and payables ledgers

To keep track of individual customer and supplier balances, it is common to maintain memorandum ledgers called the receivables ledger and the payables ledger. Each account in the receivables ledger represents the balance owed by an individual customer. Each account in the payables ledger represents the balance owed to an individual supplier.

Note that these receivables and payables ledgers **do not form part of the double entry system**.

In a computerised accounting system, the receivables ledger and the payables ledger are updated automatically when an entry is made against trade receivables or trade payables in the nominal ledger.

It is therefore very unlikely that there will be differences between the individual ledgers and the nominal ledger balances.

Discounts

> A discount is a reduction in the price of goods or services.

A supplier may have a **list** price at which it is prepared to provide its goods or services to the majority of customers. However, there may be reasons which justify a lower price or discount to particular customers or categories of customer.

It is useful to distinguish between two classes of discount:

- **Trade discount** is granted to regular customers, usually those buying in bulk quantities.
- **Early settlement discount** is granted to credit customers who pay within a specified period from the invoice date.

Accounting for early settlement discounts:

- Early settlement discounts offered to credit customers are deducted from revenue, either at the point of invoice (if the customer is expected to take advantage of the discount) or at the point of settlement of the invoice (if the customer was not originally expected to take advantage of the discount).
- Early settlement discounts received from credit suppliers are deducted from purchases either at the point of recording the invoice (if the company expects to take advantage of the discount) or at the point of payment of the invoice (if the company unexpectedly takes advantage of the discount).

Accounting for trade discounts:

- Trade discounts are deducted from revenue or purchases at the point of recording the invoice.

VAT

An indirect tax levied on the sale of goods and services

Administered by HMRC

Can have a number of rates, eg, standard rate, reduced rate

Output VAT

Sales tax charged by the business on goods/services

Output greater than input?
Pay difference to HMRC

Input greater than output?
Refund due to business

Input VAT

Sales tax on purchases made by the business

VAT and credit transactions

Sales

- Trade receivables balance includes VAT as it represents the total amount due to be received from customers.

- Sales are recorded net of (excluding VAT).

- VAT (output VAT) is recorded separately in the VAT account.

Purchases

- Trade payables balance includes VAT as it represents the total amount due to be paid to suppliers.

- Purchases are recorded net of (excluding) VAT.

- VAT (input VAT) is recorded separately in the VAT account.

Example

Trooper plc sold goods on credit to Lewis for £3,480 including VAT at 20%.

The journal entry to record the sale is:

DEBIT   Trade receivables   3,480

CREDIT Revenue   2,900

CREDIT VAT   580

VAT and cash transactions

Sales

- The amount received will represent the goods sold plus the VAT collected. This should be recorded in the cash at bank account.
- Sales are recorded net of (excluding VAT).
- VAT (output VAT) is recorded separately in the VAT account.

Purchases

- The amount paid will represent the goods purchased plus the VAT paid on those goods. This should be recorded in the cash at bank account.
- Purchases are recorded net of (excluding) VAT.
- VAT (input VAT) is recorded separately in the VAT account.

Example

Trooper Ltd sold goods to Hardeep for £4,800 including VAT at 20%. Hardeep paid in cash at the point of sale.

The journal entry to record the cash sale is:

DEBIT	Cash at bank	4,800	
CREDIT	Revenue		4,000
CREDIT	VAT		800

An example of a trial balance, incorporating the above receivables balance, is shown below.

ABC Traders Trial balance as at 30 June 20X7		
	£	£
Sales		35,000
Purchases	13,000	
Receivables	2,000	
Payables		1,500
Cash	10,000	
Capital		10,000
Loan		10,000
Rent	4,000	
Sundry expenses	3,500	
Loan interest paid	1,000	
Drawings	5,000	
Fixtures and fittings	18,000	
	56,500	56,500

Statement of profit or loss

First open up a profit or loss ledger account. Continuing our example, this ledger account is shown below, together with the rent account to illustrate how balances are transferred to it at the end of the year.

PROFIT OR LOSS				RENT			
	£		£		£		£
Purchases	13,000	Sales	35,000	Cash at bank	4,000	Profit or loss	4,000
Rent	4,000				4,000		4,000
Sundry expenses	3,500						
Loan interest	1,000						

This could be re-arranged as follows to arrive at the financial statement with which you are familiar.

ABC Traders Statement of profit or loss for the year ended 30 June 20X7	£	£
Sales		35,000
Cost of sales (here = purchases)		13,000
Gross profit		22,000
Expenses		
Rent	4,000	
Sundry expenses	3,500	
Loan interest	1,000	
		8,500
Profit for the year		13,500

Statement of financial position

The statement of financial position is prepared by following these steps:

- Balance off the accounts relating to assets and liabilities following the receivables example shown above

- Transfer the balances on the drawings account and the profit or loss ledger account (£13,500) to the capital account

> Remember to use the time available in an examination as efficiently as possible. If, for example, your statement of financial position doesn't balance, quickly check your workings, but do **not** overrun on your time allocation for the question, and do **not** worry about it. Moving on to your next question will be a much more efficient use of your time.

DRAWINGS

	£		£
Cash at bank	5,000	Capital	5,000

PROFIT OR LOSS

	£		£
Purchases	13,000	Sales	35,000
Rent	4,000		
Sundry expenses	3,500		
Loan interest	1,000		
Capital a/c	13,500		
	35,000		35,000

CAPITAL

	£		£
Drawings	5,000	Cash at bank	10,000
Balance c/d	18,500	Profit or loss	13,500
	23,500		23,500

Prepare the statement as follows:

ABC Traders
Statement of financial position as at 30 June 20X7

	£	£
Non-current assets		
Fixtures and fittings		18,000
Current assets		
Receivables	2,000	
Cash at bank	10,000	
		12,000
		30,000
Proprietor's capital		18,500
Current liabilities		
Payables	1,500	
Loan	10,000	
		11,500
		30,000

5: Preparing basic financial statements

Accounting process overview

This diagram summarises the topics you have revised so far. Look at it just before your exam – everything should fall into place.

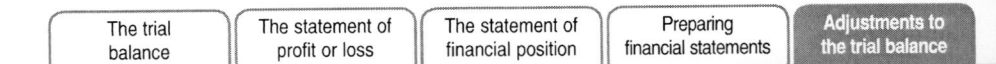

| The trial balance | The statement of profit or loss | The statement of financial position | Preparing financial statements | Adjustments to the trial balance |

Adjusting the trial balance

The initial trial balance may be adjusted for information that becomes known at or shortly after the year end or to correct errors.

The adjusted trial balance headings will look something like this.

Ledger account	Initial trial balance		Adjustments		Final trial balance	
	Dr £	Cr £	Dr £	Cr £	Dr £	Cr £

Process

1. Extract the initial trial balance from the accounting system.

2. Make the adjustments required:
   - Accruals and prepayments
   - Adjustments to inventory figures
   - Other adjustments (eg, depreciation and irrecoverable debts)

3. Check that any suspense a/c has been cleared.

4. Add the adjustments columns. Check the entries are correct and debits equal credits.

5. Add the figures across each line and record the total in the final trial balance columns.

6. Prepare the financial statements.

6: Errors and corrections to accounting records and financial statements

Topic List

Reconciliations

Types of error in accounting

The correction of errors

Suspense accounts

Trade receivables and trade payables record total amounts for all customers and suppliers. The receivables ledger and the payables ledger record the amounts owed from or to individual customers. In a computerised accounting system, the total for trade receivables will be equal to the total of the individual receivables ledger accounts at any point in time. The same is true of trade payables and the total of the payables ledger. A bank reconciliation will be carried out by a business on a regular, likely to be daily, basis. Any differences between the bank statement balance and the cash at bank balance need to be reconciled.

Although computerised systems are more accurate than manual systems, errors and omissions may still exist and require investigation and correction.

Reconciliations

It is useful to check the accuracy of what is recorded in the nominal ledgers to external documents. The most common checks are:

Supplier statement reconciliations

Suppliers will regularly (monthly or quarterly) send a statement to a customer detailing the transactions in the period and the balance at the end of the period.

The business should reconcile the statements back to the payables memorandum accounts to ensure they are consistent.

Differences should be investigated.

Bank reconciliations – computerised accounting systems and electronic banking allow bank reconciliations to be performed at any point in time, usually daily.

Bank reconciliation

A comparison of a bank statement with the cash at bank account.

The bank reconciliation is an important financial control. The bank reconciliation will invariably show a difference.

Differences on bank reconciliation

Errors: more likely in the cash at bank account.

Omissions: items on the bank statement not in the cash at bank account (eg, bank charges). Omissions require correction using a journal entry.

Timing differences: eg, payments made and entered in the cash at bank account but not yet cleared through the bank.

Proforma bank reconciliation

CASH AT BANK ACCOUNT

	£		£
Balance b/f	X	Dishonoured payment	X
Interest received	X	Bank charges	X
		Standing orders	X
		Direct debits	X
		Balance c/f	X
	$\overline{X}$		$\overline{\underline{X}}$

	£
Balance per bank statement	X
Less outstanding payments	(X)
Plus outstanding lodgements	X
Plus/less bank errors	X/(X)
Balance per adjusted cash at bank account	X

Types of error

The main types of error are as follows

- Errors of transposition, eg, writing £381 as £318 (the difference is divisible by 9)
- Errors of omission, eg, receive supplier's invoice for £500 and do not record it in the books at all
- Errors of principle, eg, treating capital expenditure as revenue expenditure
- Errors of commission, eg, putting telephone expenses of £250 in the electricity expense account
- Compensating errors, eg, both sales and purchases coincidentally incorrect by £500

Correction of errors

Errors can be corrected using a journal entry. Consider the following examples:

Example

Accountant omits to record invoice from supplier for £2,000. This would be corrected by the following journal entry:

DEBIT Purchases £2,000
CREDIT Payables £2,000

A transaction previously omitted.

Example

Accountant posts car insurance of £800 to motor vehicles account. Correct as follows:

DEBIT Motor expenses £800
CREDIT Motor vehicles £800

Correction of error of principle.